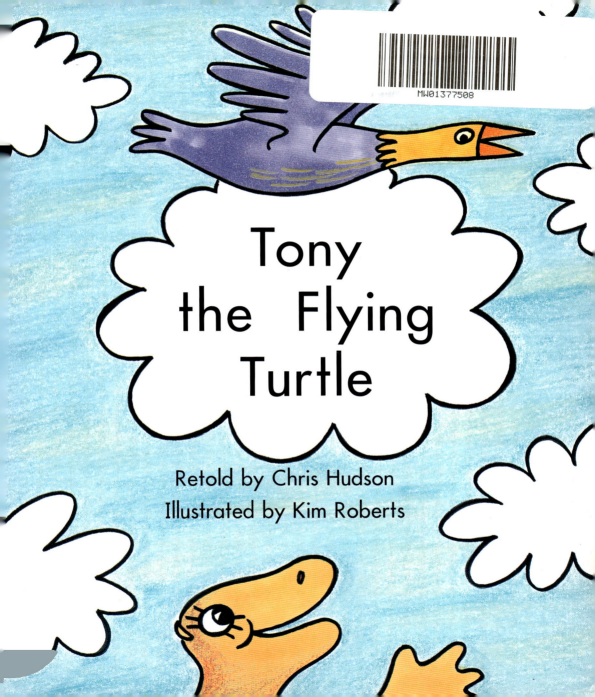

Tony the Flying Turtle

Retold by Chris Hudson
Illustrated by Kim Roberts

Tony the turtle wanted to have an adventure. "I would like to see the world," he said.

One day, Tony the turtle saw some birds in a big tree. They were very noisy and happy. "Let's go! Let's go!" they all said.

Tony said, "Hello! Where are you going?"

"We are going to fly to a warm place, far away in the south," the birds said.

Tony was excited.
"Can I come with you?"
he asked.

Tony wanted to ask,
"Where are we going?
How far is it?
When are we going to eat?"
But there was one problem.
He couldn't open his mouth.

Tony pulled his legs and his head inside his shell.

CRASH! OUCH!

His smooth shell cracked all over. Poor Tony! He was very unhappy.

Tony slowly crawled to a pond.
"I talked too much before!"
he thought.
"And now look at my shell.
It's not smooth anymore."

Soon the birds came back. "Are you going to fly with us?" they asked.

But Tony didn't say a word. "No more flying for me!" he thought.